Going Shopping

Fiona Macdonald

W
FRANKLIN WATTS
NEW YORK • LONDON • SYDNEY

This edition published 2004
© Franklin Watts 1998

First published in 1998 by
Franklin Watts
96 Leonard Street
London EC2A 4XD

Franklin Watts Australia
45-51 Huntley Street
Alexandria NSW 2015

Editor: Helen Lanz
Art Director: Robert Walster
Designer: Karen Lieberman
Consultant: Graham Upton,
Museum of Shops and
Social History, Eastbourne

ISBN 0 7496 5852 5

Printed in Malaysia

CONTENTS

Introduction

Today, people do most of their food shopping in **supermarkets**. They also go to huge **shopping centres**, where there are lots of different shops, side by side.

This is a modern supermarket that sells toys.

(Below) A toy shop around 1900.

In the past, there were no supermarkets or shopping centres. This book will tell you what it was like to go shopping many years ago.

Modern shopping centres mean people can buy all the things they want in one place.

Look at this time line. It will tell you when the photographs showing the past were taken.

Markets

Around 1900, many people did their shopping at markets.

Markets were held in the street or in special market places. Market **traders** sold their **goods** from stalls.

A street market in 1904.

A street market today.

Some people prefer shopping in markets because the prices are lower.

There are still many markets today.

Prices at markets are often cheaper than prices in shops.

City shops

Today, lots of people visit big cities to go shopping. So city streets are very busy, and city shops are crowded.

Shoppers on Oxford Street, in London, today.

It was the same long ago. City streets and shops were often busy. But many shoppers think it is busier today.

TIME LINE

1900s   1910s   1920s   1930s   1940s

Shoppers in Oxford Street, London, around 1909.
How many differences can you see between this
picture and the one on page 10?

Shoppers in the book
department of a large
store around 1900.

Department stores

Department stores are huge shops, divided into many departments. Each department sells different things.

A department store in the 1910s.

The first department stores were built in America over 100 years ago.

TIME LINE

| 1900s | **1910s** | 1920s | 1930s | 1940s |

12

Today, there are department stores in many big towns.

In department stores, it is possible to buy everything on your shopping list in one shop!

The famous London department store, Harrods, today (above) and in about 1910 (left).

Town shops

In the past, towns had lots of different shops. The shops sold everything that people needed, from food and drink to boots, blankets and bath-tubs.

Each shop sold different types of goods. **Customers** had to visit lots of different shops to buy everything on their shopping lists!

Many shops used horse-drawn carts to deliver goods to customers' homes.

(Above) A main square in a market town in the 1920s. Local people did their shopping here.

Most towns had at least one butcher's shop. This one has meat hanging outside.

1950s   1960s   1970s   1980s   1990s   2000s

Village shops

In the past, most villages had just one shop. Many village shops were very small, but they sold a lot of different things.

A village shop in the 1920s.

Village shops sold food packed in tins, bottles, boxes and jars. The packaging made sure food did not go bad if it stayed on the shelves for a long time.

TIME LINE

1900s   1910s   **1920s**   1930s   1940s

Today, some villages still have only one shop.
These village shops often sell stamps, sweets
and newspapers, as well as food. But in
many villages now there is no shop at all.

Service and display

Today, goods for sale are displayed in big, brightly-lit shop windows.

Today, customers can choose what they want to buy by looking at window displays. In the past, window displays were much smaller.

In the past, there were no **self-service** shops. Customers were served by shop **assistants**, who helped them choose what they wanted to buy.

TIME LINE

1900s   1910s   1920s   **1930s**   1940s

A food shop in the 1930s. Customers walked from *counter* to counter, buying a few things at a time.

A shoe shop in the 1930s. In the past, many goods were not displayed at all. Customers had to ask the assistant about the goods for sale.

Shopping in wartime

During the **Second World War** (which lasted from 1939 to 1945) some types of goods were difficult to find in the shops. The ships carrying them from **abroad** had been sunk by the enemy.

Many shops were destroyed by bombs in the war. So shopkeepers set up *makeshift* stalls among the ruins. This stall has managed to get some oranges and bananas to sell — a special treat!

TIME LINE

| 1900s | 1910s | 1920s | 1930s | **1940s** |

To make sure there was enough food and clothing for everyone, the government limited, or **rationed**, the amount each family could buy.

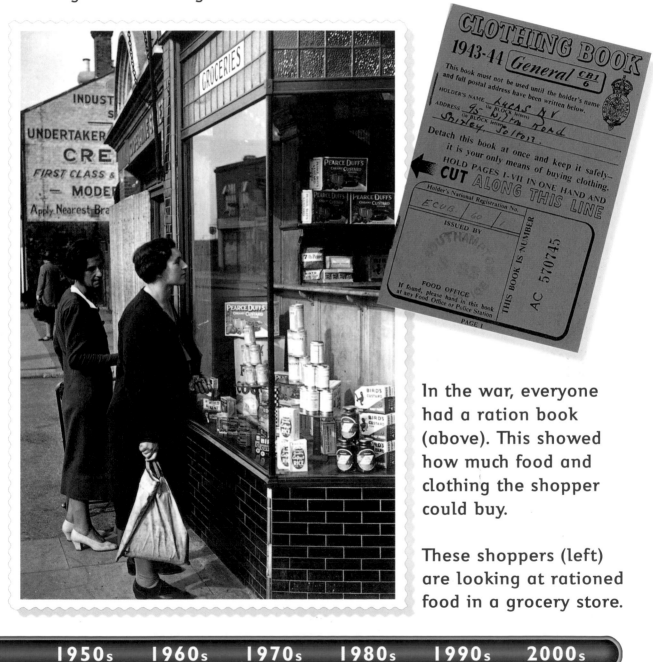

In the war, everyone had a ration book (above). This showed how much food and clothing the shopper could buy.

These shoppers (left) are looking at rationed food in a grocery store.

Shopping every day

Today, many families do their food shopping once a week. They buy lots of food, and store it in freezers and **refrigerators** until they want to eat it.

Today, shops store frozen foods in big freezers.

Frozen fish and frozen peas. In the past, these foods were bought and eaten fresh.

In the past, people went shopping every day. They did not have refrigerators or freezers so bought just enough food for each day.

TIME LINE

| 1900s | 1910s | 1920s | 1930s | 1940s |

Shopping in the 1950s.
Going shopping every
day was a good way
to meet friends and
neighbours.

Local shops

This big car park is next to a modern shopping centre. It is several miles from where the shoppers live.

Carrying shopping home, in the 1960s.

Today, many people use cars to do their shopping. They drive to **out-of-town** supermarkets and shopping centres.

Until the 1960s, many people did not have cars. They walked to the shops and carried their bags of shopping home.

TIME LINE

| 1900s | 1910s | 1920s | 1930s | 1940s |

This *shopping parade* (row of local shops) was built in the 1960s. It is close to a housing estate where many people live.

Supermarkets

Many supermarkets were built in the 1960s. They started a whole new way of shopping.

Supermarkets were often the first shops to give their customers free plastic bags to carry the goods they had bought.

In the supermarkets of the 1960s, people chose what they wanted from the shelves and paid for their goods at the checkout. It is the same in supermarkets today.

TIME LINE

| 1900s | 1910s | 1920s | 1930s | 1940s |

In the 1960s, checking out the goods took much longer than it does today. Today, *computerised* checkouts are very quick.

1950s 1960s 1970s 1980s 1990s 2000s

Useful words

abroad: from a different country.

assistant: someone who helps the customers.

computerised: when something is run by a computer.

counter: a long table in a shop. Shop assistants stand on one side, shoppers stand on the other.

customers: people who want to buy something.

goods: things that are for sale, such as food or clothes.

makeshift: made out of bits and pieces.

out-of-town: a place that is away from the town centre.

ration: to share out goods when there are not very many of them.

refrigerator: a thing that stores food at a low temperature to stop the food going bad.

Second World War: the war that lasted from 1939 to 1945. It is called a 'World War' because so many countries took part.

self-service: when customers take the goods they want off the shelves themselves and pay for them at a checkout.

shopping centres: Enormous buildings containing lots of separate shops, side by side.

shopping parade: a row of shops.

supermarkets: self-service shops that sell many different foods and drinks, and sometimes clothes and books as well.

traders: people who make a living by selling things.

Index